Presented to:

_____

By:

_____

On:

_____

To Ollie and Willie Hiemstra
and Harvis and Eunice Gemmen:
Your wisdom and love points me to God.
HG

To Richard and Rosanna Buhl:
Your desire to walk with God
always inspires me.
PW

Learn-to-Read
BIBLE

by Heather Gemmen

Peggy Wilber, General Editor

www.RocketReaders.com

Faith Kidz® is an imprint of
Cook Communications Ministries
Colorado Springs, Colorado 80918
Cook Communications, Paris, Ontario
Kingsway Communications, Eastbourne, England

LEARN-TO-READ BIBLE © 2003 by Heather Gemmen

First printing, 2003

Manufactured in China

1 2 3 4 5 6 7 8 9 10 Printing/Year 07 06 05 04 03

Illustrator: Drew Rose
Acquisitions Editor: Mary McNeil
Design Manager: Jeffrey P. Barnes
Designer: BMB Design, Inc.

Table of Contents

Old Testament

New Testament

Dear Adult,

This Bible has been created to help your child
     learn Bible stories and
     master important reading skills.

Make your reading time together even more profitable by doing **To, With,** and **By** activities (see page 13) every day to jump-start your child into fluent reading. Sit beside your child at a table or on a sofa. Help your child hold the Bible tilted up almost to eye level. (You hold one side and let your child hold the other side.)

Have your child do **To, With,** and **By** activities for only ten minutes a day. Then ask your child to reread one or two stories that he/she worked on yesterday for another ten minutes.

Encourage your child to reread a story until it sounds great and is practically memorized.

Use the comprehension question at the end of each story to begin a conversation about the Bible story your child just read.

Note: Do not make your child sound out names. Always read the name for your child if he/she stumbles over it. Think of names as freebies for your child.

To

Say to your child:

> *Listen while I read these pages **to** you.*

Read two pages out loud to your child. Run your finger under the words as you say them at a normal speed. Make sure your child is looking at the words.

With

Say to your child:

> *Read these pages **with** me.*

Read the same two pages out loud with your child. Run your finger under the words; be sure not to slow down. Your child will probably say every other word correctly.

By

Say to your child:

> *Now you read these pages **by** yourself.*

Run your finger under the words as your child says them by him/herself. Help your child fix any mistakes.

Old

Testament

Read these words to your child first:
world   dark

**God had a plan.
He made the world.
But first it was dark.**

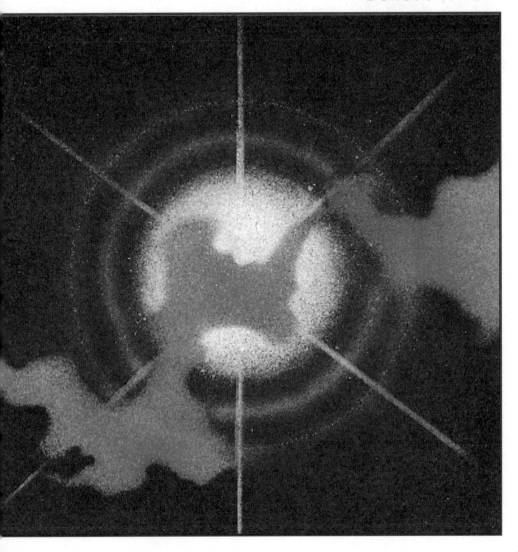

Read these words to your child first:
there   light

God said, "Let there be light."
And ka-zoom!
There was day and night.

What did God say to make day and night?

Read these words to your child first:
bigger   night

Yes, God had a plan.
God's plan was so big.
Bigger than night.
Bigger than light.

Read these words to your child first:
made   seas

God made the sky.
God made land and seas.
God made trees.

Did God have a little or a big plan?

Read these words to your child first:
How   sky

How big was God's plan?
Bigger than the sky.
Bigger than seas.

Read these words to your child first:
bright   moon

God made the sun so bright.
God made the moon so light.
God made the stars
we see at night.

What did God put in the sky?

Days Five and Six

Read these words to your child first:
Swish   birds

God made fish.
Swish!
God made birds.
Swoosh!

Read these words to your child first:
deer   turtle

**God made a deer
and a turtle.
God made all the animals.**

Can you point to the deer and the turtle?

Adam (say A-duhm)

Read these words to your child first:
very   good

God had a plan,
a very good plan.
God made a man.

Read these words to your child first:
named   lion

God named the man Adam.
Adam named the lion
and the dog.
Adam named all the animals.

What animals do you see on this page?

Read these words to your child first:
wife   glad

God made a wife.
Her name was Eve.
Adam was glad.

Read these words to your child first:

rest   good

God had a rest.
Ahhh!
Yes, God's plan was so big.
God's plan was so good.

What did God do on day seven?

The Rule

Read these words to your child first:
rule   eat

**God had a rule,
a good rule:
Do not eat from that tree
or you will die.**

Read these words to your child first:
trick   bite

**The snake had a trick,
a bad trick.
He said, "You will not die."
So Eve had a bite.
Adam had a bite.**

What was God's rule?

A Sad Day

Read these words to your child first:
snake   **lie**

The snake was bad. *Sssssss*
He said a lie. *Sssssss*
Bad snake!
God does not lie.

Read these words to your child first:
They   thing

**Adam was sad.
Eve was sad.
They did a bad thing.
God was sad, too.**

Did Adam and Eve obey or disobey God?

Cain and Abel (say Kayn, Ay-buhl)

Read these words to your child first:
gave   gift

Adam had two sons:
Cain and Abel.
Cain gave God a gift.
Abel gave God a gift.

Read these words to your child first:
best   liked

**Abel gave his best gift.
God liked that.
Cain did not give his best gift.
God did not like that.**

Read these words to your child first:
happy   thing

**Cain was not happy.
He saw Abel.
Cain did a bad thing.**

Read these words to your child first:
killed   that

Cain killed Abel.
God did not like that!

Cain did two bad things. What were they?

Noah (say Noe-uh)

Read these words to your child first:
saw   rid

God saw lots of bad men.
God was very sad.
God said, "I will get rid of all men."

Read these words to your child first:
Noah   boat

**But God saw Noah.
Noah was good.
God said to Noah, "Make a boat.
Make a big boat."**

Did Noah obey or disobey God?

Read these words to your child first:
wife   wives

**Noah and his wife
and his sons and his sons' wives
and lots of animals
got on the big boat.**

Read these words to your child first:
rain   safe

**God sent lots of rain.
But Noah and his wife
and his sons and his sons' wives
and lots of animals
were safe on the big boat.**

Why did Noah go on the boat?

Read these words to your child first:

dry   Come

The sun was out.
It was dry.
God said,
"Come out of the boat."

Read these words to your child first:
came   thanked

**Noah and his wife
and his sons and his sons' wives
and lots of animals
came out of the boat.
They thanked God.**

What do you see in the sky on this page?

Read these words to your child first:
tower   great

"Hi." "Hello." "Howdy."
"Let's make a tower.
Then we will be great!"
"This is not good," said God.
He gave the men new words.

Read these words to your child first:
These   Only

"Holá." "Bonjour." "Ciao."
These were new words.
No more tower.
Only God is great.

What happened when the men got new words?

Abraham (Say Ay-bruh-ham)

Read these words to your child first:
Abraham   loved

Abraham loved God.
God said, "Go!"
So he went.

Read these words to your child first:
went   until

**He went
and went
and went.
He went until God said, "Stop!"**

When God said, "Go!" what did Abraham do?

Your Land

Read these words to your child first:
land   kids'

**God said,
"I will give this land to you.
I will give this land to your kids.
I will give this land to your kids' kids."
But Abraham had no kids.**

Read these words to your child first:
does   lie

God said, "You will have a son."
God does not lie.
So Abraham thanked God.

What do you think happened next?

Lots of Stars

Read these words to your child first:
sky   stars

**God said,
"Look at the sky.
You will see stars.
Lots and lots of stars."**

Read these words to your child first:
family   still

**"You will have a big family.
Lots and lots of family.
As many as the stars in the sky."
But Abraham still had no kids.**

What promise did God give to Abraham?

Baby Isaac (say Ie-zak)

Read these words to your child first:
Very   old

**Abraham was old.
Very old.
And God gave him a son.**

Read these words to your child first:
Baby   Now

Baby Isaac.
Now Abraham had a son.

Do you like waiting for gifts?

Rebekah (say Re-be-kuh)

Read these words to your child first:
Isaac   grew

God had a plan for Isaac.
He grew up.

Read these words to your child first:
time   family

**It was time for him
to have a family.
But he did not have a wife.**

Read these words to your child first:
said   servant

**Abraham said to his servant,
"Go get a wife for Isaac."
The servant went.**

Read these words to your child first:

saw   Rebekah

**He went
and went
and went.
He went until he saw Rebekah.
She was the one for Isaac.**

Did the servant obey or disobey Abraham?

Esau and Jacob (say Ee-saw, Ja-kub)

Read these words to your child first:
two   twins

Isaac had not one
but two sons—twins!
Esau and Jacob.
Dad loved Esau.
Mom loved Jacob.

Read these words to your child first:
hairy   blessing

Esau liked to hunt.
Jacob did not.
Esau had hairy arms.
Jacob did not.
Esau wanted a blessing.
Uh-oh. Jacob did too.

Read these words to your child first:
made   stew

Jacob's mom had a plan.
"Get the blessing," said Jacob's mom.
"I will help you."
She made stew.
She got hair for his arms.

Read these words to your child first:
felt   ate

**Jacob went to his dad.
"I am Esau," said Jacob.
Isaac felt his hairy arms,
and he ate the stew.
"Here is the blessing," he said.**

Why did Jacob make his arms hairy?

Jacob

Read these words to your child first:

ran   away

Esau was mad!
"I will kill Jacob," he said.
Jacob ran away.
He ran and ran and ran.

Read these words to your child first:
far   dream

Jacob ran far away.
"You will be back,"
God said to him in a dream.
God had a plan for Jacob.

Did you know God speaks to people in dreams?

Read these words to your child first:
many   twelve

Jacob had many sons.
Not one. Not two.
Not three.
Jacob had twelve sons.
But he loved Joseph best.

Read these words to your child first:
nice   coat

Jacob made a nice coat.
He did not make twelve,
or three, or two.
He made one coat for Joseph.

Read these words to your child first:
great   brothers

**"I had a dream
that I will be great,"
Joseph said to his brothers.
They got mad.**

Read these words to your child first:
sold   slave

They put him in a well.
They sold him.
Joseph was a slave.
But God had a plan for him.

What is often at the bottom of a well?

In Jail

Read these words to your child first:
Joseph   taken

Joseph was taken
out of the well.
He was taken far away.
And God was with him.

Read these words to your child first:
asked   jail

**A woman asked Joseph
to do a bad thing.
He said, "No."
She got mad.
She made Joseph go to jail.**

Read these words to your child first:
God   plan

But God had a plan for him.

Read these words to your child first:
dreams   true

"We had dreams," said two men.
"I can tell you what they mean,"
said Joseph.
The dreams came true.

How do you think Joseph knew what the
dreams meant?

More Dreams

Read these words to your child first:
king   help

"I had dreams," said the king.
"Joseph can help,"
said a man from the jail.

Read these words to your child first:
food   **ready**

**"God can help," said Joseph.
"God says there will be lots of food.
Then there will be no food.
So get ready."**

What should the king do to get ready?

Big Boss

Read these words to your child first:
Other   none

The king made Joseph boss
of all the land.
Joseph was a good boss.
Soon his land had lots of food.
Other lands had none.

Read these words to your child first:
came   who

**Then, not one,
not two, not three,
but ten brothers
came to get food.
Joseph did not tell them
who he was.**

Read these words to your child first:
Later   eleven

**Later, not one,
not two, not three,
but eleven brothers
came to get food.**

Read these words to your child first:
told   them

Joseph told them who he was.
He was not mad.
He was glad.
He said, "God had a plan for us."

Did Joseph punish or forgive his brothers?

Baby Moses (say Moe-zis)

Read these words to your child first:
Years   died

Years **later**,
after Joseph **died**,
a new king had a plan.
He had a bad plan.

Read these words to your child first:
Kill   boys

**"Kill the baby boys
of Abraham
and Isaac
and Jacob's big family."**

Read these words to your child first:
die   princess

One baby boy did not die.
The princess took him.

Read these words to your child first:
baby   Moses

He was baby Moses.
God had a plan for him.

Where did the princess find baby Moses?

Moses

Read these words to your child first:
grew   mean

**Moses grew up.
The king was mean
to Abraham
and Isaac
and Jacob's big family.**

Read these words to your child first:
people   help

**The king was mean to God's people.
"Go," God said to Moses.
"Go help my people."**

Read these words to your child first:
can't   save

"Not me!" said Moses.
"I can't save them,"
"I can," said God.
"Go!"

Read these words to your child first:
Moses   king

**He went
and went
and went.
Moses went to see the king.**

See the burning bush? God talked to
Moses from the burning bush.

Let Them Go

Read these words to your child first:
God's   people

"Let them go," said Moses.
"Let God's people go."

Read these words to your child first:
said   **them**

"No," said the king.
"I will **not** let **them** go."
But God had a plan.

Read these words to your child first:
frogs   more

God sent frogs.
He sent bugs.
He did more.

Read these words to your child first:

flies   hail

God sent flies.
He sent hail.
He did more.
But the king did not let them go.

What is hail?

Read these words to your child first:
blood   doors

"I will do one more thing,"
God said to Moses.
"Tell my people
to put sheep blood on the doors."

Read these words to your child first:
every   house

**God killed the first son
in every house
that did not have blood on the door.
The king said, "Go!"**

Why did the people put blood on the doors?

A Path

Read these words to your child first:
God's   people

**God's people went
and went
and went.
Moses went too.**

Read these words to your child first:
What   done

"What **have** we **done**?"
said the king.
"I want them back."
The king and his men
went after Moses.

Read these words to your child first:
Yikes   after

**"Yikes!" said God's people.
"The king is after us.
We will die."**

**"Do not be afraid," said Moses.
"God will save us."
And he did.
God made a path in the sea.**

Where is Moses?

Good Water

Read these words to your child first:
Yikes   water

"Yikes!" said God's people.
"We have no water.
We will die."

Read these words to your child first:
Obey   save

"Obey me," said God.
"I will save you."
And he did.
He gave them good water.

Does God take care of his people?

Good Food

Read these words to your child first:
food   die

**"Yikes!" said God's people.
"We have no food.
We will die."**

Read these words to your child first:
Trust   manna

**"Trust me," said God.
"I will give you food."
And he did.
He sent meat and manna.**

What do you say when someone gives you food?

Hard Work

Read these words to your child first:
work   hard

"Moses, you work hard
for God's people," said a man.

Read these words to your child first:
need   help

"You work too hard," he said.
"You need help."
So Moses got help.

Did Moses listen to the man?

Good Rules

Read these words to your child first:
came   mountain

**Moses and God's people
came to a mountain.
Moses went up to God.
Up.
Up.
Up.**

Read these words to your child first:
good   rules

God gave Moses ten good rules.
Moses went down.
Down.

Down.

Down.

Read these words to your child first:
Moses   told

**Moses told God's people
the good rules.**

Read these words to your child first:
what   **says**

"Yes!
We will do what God says,"
said God's people.

Read these words to your child first:
not   sin

**Moses said,
"God gave us rules
so we will not sin."**

Read these words to your child first:
God's **people**

"We are God's people,"
said Moses.
"God has a good plan for us."

Why did God make rules?

Into the Land

Read these words to your child first:
Send   some

**God said, "Send some men
to the land I will give you."**

Read these words to your child first:
Twelve   afraid

Twelve men went into the land.
They saw BIG men.
Ten men were afraid.
Two men were not afraid.

Read these words to your child first:
trust   time

**God was mad
that ten men did not trust him.
"You will not get this land,"
God said.
"Not for a long time."**

Read these words to your child first:

later **with**

A long time later,
God sent them to the land.
"I am with you," God said.

Why did God's people have to wait a long
time to get the land?

March!

Read these words to your child first:
town   yours

**"This town is yours," God said.
"I will give it to you."**

Read these words to your child first:
march   around

"March around it," said God.
They did.
March, march.
They blew the horns.
Toot, toot!
They did this for six days.

Read these words to your child first:
seven   more

**On day seven,
God said to march some more.
They did.
March, march.
Seven times around.**

Read these words to your child first:
walls   down

TOOT, TOOT!
The walls fell down.
God gave the town to them.

Did the people obey or disobey God?

Happy People

Read these words to your child first:
many   towns

God gave them **many towns.**
God's people were happy.
God's plan was good.

Read these words to your child first:
rules   awhile

They sang lots of songs.
They ate lots of food.
They did God's rules
for awhile . . .

What does "for awhile" mean?

Help!

Read these words to your child first:
forgot   them

Then they forgot God.
Uh-oh.
God was mad.
He let bad men get them.

Read these words to your child first:
they   cried

**"Help!" they cried to God.
"Help, help!"**

Does God help his people?

Deborah (say Deb-ruh)

Read these words to your child first:
family   Abraham

**God did help.
He did not want the big family
of Abraham, Isaac, and Jacob
to be sad.**

Read these words to your child first:
Deborah   beat

God sent Deborah to help.
He told her how to
beat the bad men.

Read these words to your child first:
fight war

"Go fight,"
she said to God's people.
"You will win the war."

Read these words to your child first:
rules   awhile

And they did.
God was with them.
They did God's rules
for awhile . . .

Who did God send to help?

Gideon (say Gi-dee-uhn)

Read these words to your child first:
forgot   Again

**But they forgot God.
Again.
God was sad.
He let bad men get them.**

Read these words to your child first:
Gideon   fight

**"Help!" they cried to God.
"Help, help!"
And he did.
He sent Gideon to help.
"Go fight," said God.**

Read these words to your child first:
many   home

"You have too many men," said God.
Some men went home.
"I will save you with less men,"
said God.

Read these words to your child first:
rules   awhile

And he did.
God was with them.
They did God's rules
for awhile . . .

What are the men carrying in these pictures?

Samson (say Sam-suhn)

Read these words to your child first:
again   Samson

But they forgot God.
Oh, no. Not again!
God let bad men get them.
"Help, help!" they cried to God.
God sent Samson to help.

Read these words to your child first:
hair   strong

**God said, "You will be strong
if you do not cut your hair."
A woman cut his hair.
He was weak.**

Read these words to your child first:
jail   grew

Bad men put him in jail.
His hair grew.
God made him strong again.

Read these words to your child first:
Bring   killed

"**Bring** out Samson," said the bad men.
They made fun of him.
He asked God for help.
Then he **killed** the bad men.

Why was Samson strong?

Naomi (say Nay-o-mee)

Read these words to your child first:
husband   alone

Naomi's husband died.
Her sons died.
She was sad.
But she was not alone.

Read these words to your child first:
took   care

"I will go with you,"
said Ruth.
She took care of Naomi.

Read these words to your child first:
married   Ruth

A good man married Ruth.
He took care of
Ruth and Naomi.

Read these words to your child first:
baby   this

Ruth had a baby.
Ruth and Naomi took care
of the baby.
This was God's plan.

Are babies part of God's plan?

Hannah (say Ha-nuh)

Read these words to your child first:
wanted   **Please**

Hannah wanted a baby.
"Please give me a baby,"
she said to God.

Read these words to your child first:
give   God's

"If you give me a baby,
I will give my baby to you,"
she said to God.
"Let it be," said God's man.

Read these words to your child first:
gave   Samuel

**God gave her a baby.
The baby was Samuel.**

Read these words to your child first:
grew house

Samuel grew to be a boy.
Hannah let Samuel live
in God's house.

Did God give Hannah what she wanted?

Samuel (say Sam-yool)

Read these words to your child first:
voice   God's

"Samuel!" said a voice.
Was it God's man?
No.

Read these words to your child first:
again   talked

"Samuel!" said the voice again.
Was it God's man?
No.
It was God.
God talked to Samuel.

Are you glad that God talks to his people?

David (say Day-vid)

Read these words to your child first:
grew   Jesse's

Samuel grew up.
God said to Samuel,
"Go find a new king.
Go find Jesse's son."
Samuel went.

Read these words to your child first:
first   second

**He saw Jesse's sons.
Was Jesse's first son the new king?
No.
Was Jesse's second son the new king?
No.**

Read these words to your child first:
seven   another

**He saw seven sons.
No, no, no, no, no, no, no.
"Do you have another son?"
said Samuel.**

Read these words to your child first:
sheep   came

"Yes. He is with the sheep,"
said Jesse.
"Let me see him," said Samuel.
David came.
"He is the one," said God.

Why did Samuel want to see David?

Good Music

Read these words to your child first:
Saul   play

**King Saul felt bad.
"Get David," said King Saul.
"He will play for me."**

Read these words to your child first:
David's   good

David's music was good.
King Saul was glad.

What instrument is David playing?

A Big Man

Read these words to your child first:
care   clang

David took care of sheep.
His brothers went to war.

Read these words to your child first:
David **brothers**

**Jesse said to David,
"Go to your brothers."
David went.**

Read these words to your child first:
afraid   beat

David saw a big man.
A big, bad man.
David was not afraid.
"God will beat you!"
he said.

Read these words to your child first:
people   safe

And God did.
God's people were safe.

Why was David not afraid of the big man?

Jonathan (say Jon-uh-thuhn)

Read these words to your child first:
loved   coat

**King Saul had a son
named Jonathan.
Jonathan loved David.
He gave David a coat.**

Read these words to your child first:
people   that

The **people** loved David.
The **people** loved David
more than they loved King Saul.
King Saul did not like that.

Read these words to your child first:
David   Jonathan

"Kill David," the king said.
"No!" said Jonathan.
"Do not kill David."

Read these words to your child first:
All   right

**"All right," said the king.
"I will not kill David."**

What was the name of King Saul's son?

Read these words to your child first:
lie   chase

Did the king lie?
Yes.
Did the king chase David?
Yes.

Read these words to your child first:
kill   with

Did the king kill David?
No.
God was with David.

Read these words to your child first:
fell   asleep

**The king fell asleep.
"Let me kill the king,"
a man said.
"No," said David.
"Do not kill the king."**

Read these words to your child first:
David **woke**

David woke the king.
"I did not kill you," said David.
"You were good," said the king.
"I was bad."

Why didn't David kill the king?

Read these words to your child first:
gone   When

**David and his men went away.
When they came back,
their cows were gone
and their kids were gone.**

Read these words to your child first:
catch   their

**David said to God,
"Will we catch the bad men?"
God said, "Yes."
They got their kids back.
They got their cows back.**

What is David doing in this picture?

Hurt Legs

Read these words to your child first:
died   Jonathan's

King Saul died.
Jonathan died.
Jonathan's son had to run away.

Read these words to your child first:
hurt   alive

His nurse took him and ran.
Faster. Faster. Faster.
Oh, no. He fell.
His legs were hurt, but he was alive.

How did the boy hurt his legs?

161

David Is King

Read these words to your child first:
people   asked

**God's people
asked David to be king.**

Read these words to your child first:
This   God's

King David!
This was God's plan.

What is on David's head that helps you
know he is king?

Jonathan's Son

Read these words to your child first:
many   gone

**David was king for many years.
He was sad that Saul was gone.
He was sad that Jonathan was gone.**

Read these words to your child first:
each   other

"I want to see Jonathan's son,"
he said.
"I want to take care of him."
They were happy to see each other.

What is the opposite of sad?

A Good King

Read these words to your child first:
loved   times

**David was a good king.
He loved God in bad times.
He loved God in good times.**

Read these words to your child first:
make   **temple**

**"I want to make a temple for God.
A big, big temple," said David.
God said, "Let your son make it."
David said, "Yes, God.
I will let him make it."**

What is a temple?

167

Good Songs

Read these words to your child first:
songs   **sang**

**King David wrote
good songs to God.
He sang good songs to God.**

Read these words to your child first:
God's   people

**God's people sang songs
to God.**

Can you sing a song to God?

Solomon (say So-luh-muhn)

Read these words to your child first:
dream   anything

**David's son Solomon was king.
He had a dream.
God said,
"I will give you anything you ask."**

Read these words to your child first:
money   wise

**Did Solomon ask God for a long life?
No.
Did he ask God for lots of money?
No.
He said to God, "Help me to be wise."**

Why is it good for a king to be wise?

God's Temple

Read these words to your child first:
helped   gave

God helped him to be wise
and
God gave him long life
and
God gave him lots of money.

Read these words to your child first:
make   temple

"I will make God's temple,"
said Solomon.

Read these words to your child first:
years   thirteen

**It took a long time.
Not one year.
Not two years.
It took thirteen years
to make God's temple.**

Read these words to your child first:
beautiful   how

It was big.
It was beautiful.
It was just how God wanted it.

Why did it take so long to build the temple?

A Big Party

Read these words to your child first:
done   Solomon

The work was all done.
Yes!
Solomon prayed to God.
He said, "There is no God like you."

Read these words to your child first:
party   happy

**God's people had a party.
A big party.
God's people sang songs to God.
They were happy.**

Why did they have a party?

Too Many Wives

Read these words to your child first:
brown   **white**

Solomon had lots of wives.
Some were brown.
Some were white.
Some were short.
Some were tall.

Read these words to your child first:
loved   other

**Some loved God.
Some didn't.
They loved other gods.**

Read these words to your child first:
There   prayed

Solomon loved his wives.
He forgot, "There is no God like you."
He prayed to other gods.
That was bad.

Read these words to your child first:
little   part

**God was mad.
He said to Solomon,
"Your son will not be king of all the land.
He will get a little part of the land."**

Why was God unhappy with Solomon?

Elijah (say Ee-lie-juh)

Read these words to your child first:
Ahab   rain

Elijah was God's man.
He said to bad King Ahab,
"It will not rain."

Read these words to your child first:
birds   bring

**And it did not rain
for a long, long time.
God sent birds
to bring food to Elijah.**

Why did God took care of Elijah?

More Food

Read these words to your child first:
Later   widow

**Later, Elijah said to a widow,
"Please give me some food."
She said, "I do not have much food."**

Read these words to your child first:
some   more

**Elijah said to the widow,
"God will not let you run out of food."
She gave him some food.
Then she had more food!
God did not let the food run out.**

What is a widow?

He Is Alive!

Read these words to your child first:
widow's   **sick**

The widow's son got sick.
Her son died.
She was sad.

Read these words to your child first:
asked   alive

Elijah asked God for help.
God gave the boy life.
"He's alive!" Elijah said to her.
"You are God's man!" she said.

Can you tell this story in your own words?

Send Fire

Read these words to your child first:
loved   other

**King Ahab did not love God.
He loved other gods.
His men loved other gods.**

Read these words to your child first:
Elijah   **fire**

**Elijah said to bad King Ahab,
"Can your god send fire?"
"Yes," said the bad king.**

189

Read these words to your child first:
danced   yelled

The king's men sang.
No fire.
The king's men danced.
No fire.
The king's men yelled.
No fire.

Read these words to your child first:
sleeping   **Lord**

"Your god is sleeping," said Elijah.
He asked God to send fire.
And God sent fire.
The people said, "The Lord is God!"

Do you think God ever sleeps?

Was It God?

Read these words to your child first:
queen   afraid

The bad queen was mad.
"I will kill you," she said to Elijah.
He was afraid.
He ran away.

Read these words to your child first:
sleep   angel

**He went to sleep.
God sent an angel with some food.
He felt better.
"But they want to kill me,"
he said to God.**

Read these words to your child first:
there   wind

"Go up there,"
God said to Elijah.
"I will pass by."
A big wind came.
Was it God?
No.

Read these words to your child first:
earthquake   whisper

An earthquake came. Was it God?
No.
A fire came. Was it God?
No.
God was in a whisper.
God took care of Elijah.

Is God stronger than the bad queen?

Ahab (say Ay-hab)

Read these words to your child first:
buy   your

Ahab was a bad king.
"I want more land," he said.
"I want to buy your land."

Read these words to your child first:
family   years

"No," said the man.
"My **family** has had this land
for **years**
and **years**
and **years**."

Read these words to your child first:
home   Hmph

"I want this land," Ahab said.
He went home mad.
Hmph!

Read these words to your child first:
queen   killed

"Do not be mad," said the queen.
The queen killed the man.
Ahab took the land.

Do you think God was happy with Ahab?

Elisha (say Ee-lie-shuh)

Read these words to your child first:
Elijah   Elisha

**Elijah was God's man.
He was old.
Elisha was God's man.
He was young.**

Read these words to your child first:
there   too

Elijah said, "I will go there."
Elisha said, "I will go there, too."
Elijah went.
Elisha went, too.

Read these words to your child first:
What   Spirit

"**What** can I do for you?" Elijah said.
"Let me have God's **Spirit**,"
said Elisha.
"If you see me go, it will be so,"
said Elijah.

Read these words to your child first:
with saw

Elijah went to be with God.
Elisha saw him go.
Now Elisha had God's Spirit.

What did Elisha want from Elijah?

Will We Win?

Read these words to your child first:
friend   loved

**King Ahab was a bad king.
He did not love God.
His friend was a good king.
He loved God.**

Read these words to your child first:
help   other

Ahab said to his friend,
"Will you help me
kill some bad men?"
"Yes," said the other king,
"if God says we will win."

Read these words to your child first:
God's   Say

**"Will we win?" Ahab said to God's man.
"Say yes!"
"God says, 'No!'" said God's man.**

Read these words to your child first:
right   killed

King Ahab was mad.
But God's man was right.
They did not win.
Ahab was killed.

What is the opposite of win?

Dead Men

Read these words to your child first:
coming   king's

"Bad men are coming,"
the king's men said
to the good king.
Yikes!

Read these words to your child first:
What   afraid

"What will we do?"
the good king said to God.
God said, "Do not be afraid.
Go to the bad men."
God had a plan.

Read these words to your child first:
king   king's

The king went.
The king's men went.
They went
and went
and went.

Read these words to your child first:
each   other

They got to the bad men.
The bad men were dead.
The bad men killed each other!

Did God help the good king?

Lots of Oil

Read these words to your child first:
money widow

"I have no money,"
said a widow.
"I have no food."

Read these words to your child first:
little   oil

**"All I have is a little oil," she said.
"God will help," said Elisha.
And God did.
God made the little oil into lots of oil.**

What do you think the widow did with the oil?

Get Better

Read these words to your child first:
sick   well

A man was sick.
"He can get well," said a girl.
"He can get well?" said his wife.

Read these words to your child first:
You   wife

**"You can get well!" said the wife.
"I can get well?" said the man.**

Who do you think will make him well?

Read these words to your child first:
said   girl

**"Go to God's man,"
said the girl.
He went.**

Read these words to your child first:

dip   river

"Go dip in the river,"
said God's man.
He went.
God made him well.

What does "dip in the river" mean?

Joash (say Joe-ash)

Read these words to your child first:

mean   queen

A king died.
His mom was queen.
She killed the king's sons.
She was mean.
She was a mean queen.

Read these words to your child first:
killed   grew

One son was not killed: Joash.
He grew up.
He loved God.
"I am king,"
said Joash to the mean queen.

Do you think God had a plan for Joash?

Hezekiah (say He-ze-kie-uh)

Read these words to your child first:
house   dirty

Hezekiah was a good king.
"God's house is dirty," he said.
"Let's clean his house.
Let's love God."

Read these words to your child first:
people   **clean**

"Yes!" the people said
to the king.
"We will clean God's house.
We will love God."

Read these words to your child first:
house   **people**

"Go to God's house," said the king.
The people went.
They went
and went
and went.

Read these words to your child first:
thank   happy

**They went to see God's clean house.
They sang songs.
They said thank you to God.
God was happy with his people.**

What can you do today that will
make God happy?

Prayer

Read these words to your child first:
Hezekiah   Very

King Hezekiah was sick.
Very, very sick.
"You will die," said God.
It was God's plan.

Read these words to your child first:
don't   die

**The king was sad.
Very, very sad.
"Oh, God, don't let me die," he said.
"You will not die now," said God.
It was God's new plan.**

Why did God change his plan?

God's Words

Read these words to your child first:
Read   words

"Read my words to the people,"
God said to his man.
"They may be sad
that they have been bad."

Read these words to your child first:
Were   fire

Were the people sad?
No!
The king put God's words in the fire.
The king was bad.

Why do you think the king put
God's words in the fire?

In the Fire

Read these words to your child first:
bow   three

"We will not bow to your god," three men said to the bad king.

Read these words to your child first:
won't   save

"You won't bow?" said the king.
"I will kill you."
"We won't bow," they said.
"God can save us."

Read these words to your child first:
Put   die

"Put them in the fire!"
said the king.
The king's men put them in the fire.
Did they die?

Read these words to your child first:
angel   save

No!
God sent an angel.
Did God save them?
Yes!

Can you tell this story in your own words?

Daniel (say Dan-yul)

Read these words to your child first:
make   rule

"Let's make a plan,"
said the king's bad men.
"Let's get rid of Daniel."
"Oh, king," they said,
"make a rule."

Read these words to your child first:
that   praying

"Make a rule that
all people must pray to you."
"Yes," said the king.
"Oh, king," said the bad men,
"Daniel is praying to God."

Read these words to your child first:
rid   rule

**"Get rid of Daniel,"
said the bad men.
"It is a rule."**

Read these words to your child first:
put   lions'

**The king put Daniel in the lions' den.
Did God save Daniel?
Yes!**

Is God stronger than hungry lions?

Fix the Walls

Read these words to your child first:
your   want

"Oh, God," said God's man,
"we are your people.
We have been bad.
We want to be good."

Read these words to your child first:
city   trouble

"Oh, God," said God's man,
"our city is in trouble.
Will you help us
fix the walls of our city?"

Read these words to your child first:
worked   work

**God's people worked
on the walls.
Bang, bang.
Clang, clang.
It was hard work.**

Read these words to your child first:
tried   them

Bad men tried to stop them.
But God helped them.
The walls went up.

Do you think they finished building the walls?

Ezra (say Ez-ruh)

Read these words to your child first:
done   near

**The walls were done.
God's man read
God's words
to God's people
near the tall walls.**

Read these words to your child first:
seven **Praise**

**He read
and read and read.
He read for seven days.
"Praise God," said Ezra.
"Amen," said the people.**

What does "Praise God" mean?

Esther (say Es-ter)

Read these words to your child first:
looking   wife

**The king was looking
for a wife.**

Read these words to your child first:
king **Cousin**

**Esther went to the king.
"Bye, Cousin!"
She went to be the king's wife.**

What is the wife of a king called?

The King's Bad Man

Read these words to your child first:
hate   people

"I hate God's people,"
said the king's bad man.
"Let me kill them,"
he said to the king.
"Yes," said the king.

Read these words to your child first:
Esther's   cousin

Esther's cousin was sad.
Very, very sad.
"We are God's people,"
he said. "We will die."

Read these words to your child first:
wants   Who

"Oh, King," said Esther,
"a bad man wants to kill my people."
"Who is the bad man?"
said the king.

Read these words to your child first:
your   die

"He is your man," said Esther.
The king was mad.
"No," he said.
"God's people will not die.
The bad man will die."

Does God love his people?

Jonah (say Joe-nuh)

Read these words to your child first:
people   good

"Go," God said to Jonah.
"Tell the people to be good."
Jonah went.
He went
and went and went.

Read these words to your child first:
away **Throw**

He went **away** from the people!
He got in a boat.
God sent a storm.
"God is mad at me," said Jonah.
"**Throw** me in."

249

Read these words to your child first:
Down   fish

Jonah went down.
Down.
Down.
Down.
God sent a fish.

Read these words to your child first:
two   sorry

Jonah was in the fish.
Not for one day.
Not for two days.
He was in the fish for three days.
He was sorry.

Read these words to your child first:
prayed   spit

He prayed to God.
God made the
fish spit Jonah out.
"Go," God said to Jonah.

Read these words to your child first:
told   people

**Jonah went.
He went
and went
and went.
He told the people to be good.**

What does sorry mean?

A Bright Light

Read these words to your child first:
Again   **told**

God's people were bad.
Again.
But God had a plan.
A BIG plan.
God told his plan to his man.

Read these words to your child first:
dark   **light**

"My people are in the dark.
But a baby will be born.
He will be a light.
He will be a light to all people."

Do you know who the baby is?

255

The New Testament

John (say Jon)

Read these words to your child first:
angel   woman

"You will have a baby,"
an angel said
to an old man
and an old woman.

Read these words to your child first:
name **ready**

"His name will be John,"
said the angel.
"He will help people
get ready for the Lord."

Do old men and old women usually have babies?

Read these words to your child first:
have   baby

The angel went to Mary, too.
"You will have a baby," he said.
"Me?" said Mary.
"Yes, you," said the angel.

Read these words to your child first:
Son   Jesus

**"He will be God's Son,"
said the angel.
"His name will be Jesus."
"Let it be," said Mary.**

What good news did the angel tell Mary?

261

The Lord

Read these words to your child first:
shepherds   news

**The angel went to some shepherds.
He did not say, "You will have a baby."
He said, "I have good news!"**

Read these words to your child first:
manger   Lord

"A baby is born," said the angel.
"You will see him in a manger.
He is the Lord."

Read these words to your child first:
baby **shepherds**

**"Let's go see the baby,"
said the shepherds.**

Read these words to your child first:
They   saw

They saw baby Jesus.
They saw God's Son.

What do animals do at a manger?

Wise Men

Read these words to your child first:
wise   star

**The angel did not go to the wise men.
The wise men saw a star.
"The star of a king!" they said.**

Read these words to your child first:
until   Jesus

"Let's go see the king,"
said the wise men.
They went
and went and went.
They went until they saw Jesus.

Read these words to your child first:

gifts   wise

**"We bring gifts for the king,"
said the wise men.**

Read these words to your child first:
Kings   Lords

Jesus is King of Kings.
Jesus is Lord of Lords.

Can you name one gift the men gave to Jesus?
Hint: What color jewelry are they wearing?

Give Thanks

Read these words to your child first:
seen   held

**"I have seen the Lord,"
said God's man.
He held baby Jesus.**

Read these words to your child first:
Give   **thanks**

**"Give thanks to God,"
said God's woman.**

When you are happy, do you remember
to thank God, too?

A Bad King

Read these words to your child first:
kill   Joseph

A bad king had a bad plan—
to kill Jesus.
But God had a good plan.
"Go," he said to Joseph.
"Go far away."

Read these words to your child first:
Jesus   away

Joseph and Mary and Jesus went.
They went
and went and went.
They went until they got away
from the king.

What animal is Mary and Jesus riding on?

273

A Good Son

Read these words to your child first:
bigger   happy

**Jesus grew bigger
and bigger.
He was good.
His mom and dad were happy.**

Read these words to your child first:

helped   work

Jesus helped Joseph at work.

Joseph was a carpenter.
What does a carpenter do?

Lost!

Read these words to your child first:
twelve **family**

**When Jesus was twelve,
his family went to God's house.**

Read these words to your child first:
home   lost

**When his family went home,
Jesus did not go with them.
Was he lost?**

Read these words to your child first:
Where   Jesus

"Where is Jesus?" said Mary.
"Where is Jesus?" said Joseph.

Read these words to your child first:
talking **about**

They went back to God's house.
Jesus was in God's house.
He was talking to wise men about God.

Why do you think Jesus was in God's house?

God's Word

Read these words to your child first:
read **God's**

Jesus read God's Word.
He read
and read
and read.

Read these words to your child first:
things   heart

**He read good things in God's Word.
"Love the Lord your God
with all your heart."**

What book do we call God's Word?

The Lord Is Here!

Read these words to your child first:
ready   coming

John grew up.
He said to lots of people,
"Get ready.
The Lord is coming."

John 1:29–34

Read these words to your child first:
John   here

**Jesus grew up.
"Look," said John.
"The Lord is here.
Jesus is God's Son!"**

What does "Get ready!" mean?

283

Read these words to your child first:
would   heal

God's Word said
that God would send someone
to heal the sick
and save the people.

Read these words to your child first:
Then   sent

**Jesus read God's Word
to the people.
Then he said,
"I am the one God sent."**

How do you know that Jesus is good?

Come With Me

Read these words to your child first:
some   three

"Come with me," said Jesus.
"Yes," said some men.
Not one man.
Not two men.
Not three men.

Read these words to your child first:
Twelve   work

**Twelve men said yes.
"Do my work with me," said Jesus.
"Yes," they said.**

Why did the men want to help Jesus do his work?

Be Still!

Read these words to your child first:
came   Splash

Jesus and his men sat in a boat.
A BIG wind came.
Whooooo!
A BIG wave came.
Splash!

Read these words to your child first:
storm   still

**"Yikes!" said the men.
"A storm! We will die!"
Jesus got up.
"Be still," he said.
The wind and waves were still.**

Why could Jesus tell the storm to be still?   **289**

Big Faith

Read these words to your child first:
servant   heal

"My servant is sick,"
a man said to Jesus.
"I will go and heal him,"
said Jesus.

Read these words to your child first:
word   well

"Lord, you do not need to go,"
said the man.
"Just say a word
and he will be well."

Read these words to your child first:
Wow   faith

"Wow!" said Jesus.
"Your faith is big."

Read these words to your child first:
home   servant

**"Go home," said Jesus.
"Your servant will be well."
And he was!**

Do you believe that Jesus can heal people
with just a word?

Body and Soul

Read these words to your child first:
Many   friend

**Many people went to see Jesus.
"There are too many people,"
said four men with a sick friend.**

Read these words to your child first:
Through   roof

"We can't see Jesus.
Jesus can't see our friend.
"Put him through the roof!" they said.

Read these words to your child first:
forgive   sins

**Jesus said to the man,
"I forgive your sins.
Take up your mat and go home."
The man went home.**

Read these words to your child first:
body   soul

**The man's body was well
and
the man's soul was well.
Jesus made him well.**

What does "soul" mean?

Happy Family

Read these words to your child first:
Please   come

A man went to Jesus.
He was sad.
"My little girl is sick," he said.
"Please come."

Read these words to your child first:
they   died

**Jesus went.
As they went, the girl died.
Did Jesus stop?**

Read these words to your child first:
still   went

No.
He still went to the girl.

Read these words to your child first:
Little   girl

**Jesus said, "Little girl, get up."
The girl got up.**

Why was the family happy?

Happy Man

Read these words to your child first:
hear   talk

"Jesus," said some men,
"help him.
He can't hear.
He can't talk."

Read these words to your child first:
Open   could

"Open up," said Jesus.
The man could hear.
The man could talk.

Was the man "deaf" or "death"?

Mary and Martha (say Mar-thuh)

Read these words to your child first:
went   worked

Jesus went to see Mary and Martha.
Mary sat by Jesus.
She sat and sat.
Martha did not sit.
She worked and worked.

Read these words to your child first:
wants   **hear**

"Jesus," said Martha.
"Tell Mary to help me."
"Martha, Martha," said Jesus.
"You work too much.
Mary wants to hear me. That is good."

Which sister listened to Jesus?

305

The Throne

Read these words to your child first:
Someday   throne

**"Someday I will sit on my throne,"
said Jesus.
"I will say 'Come' to all who love me."**

Read these words to your child first:
kind   others

**"'How did we love you?'
my people will ask.
I will say,
'When you were kind to others
you were kind to me.'"**

How can you be kind to someone today?

Be Great

Read these words to your child first:
table   spot

**Jesus sat by a table.
Some men sat by the table.
"I get the good spot," said a man.
"No, I get the good spot,"
said all the men.**

Read these words to your child first:
there   great

**"Do not try to sit at the good spot,"
said Jesus.
"Let other people sit there.
Then you will be great."**

What does it mean to be great?

309

A Better Prayer

Read these words to your child first:
pray   better

Two men went to God's house to pray.
One man said,
"Dear God, I am good.
I am so good.
I am better than other people."

Read these words to your child first:
other   forgive

**The other man said,
"Dear God, I am bad.
I am so bad.
Will you forgive me?"
God was happy with this man.**

What does forgive mean?

311

The Best Prayer

Read these words to your child first:
things   give

"Ask God for good things,
and he will **give** them to you,"
Jesus said to his men.

Read these words to your child first:
show   pray

**"Do not show off when you pray,"
Jesus said.
"Pray to God like this:**

Read these words to your child first:
heaven   kingdom

"Our Father in heaven,
holy be your name,
your kingdom come,
your will be done
on earth as it is in heaven.
Give us today our daily bread.

Read these words to your child first:

Forgive   temptation

**Forgive us our sins
as we forgive other people.
Lead us not into temptation,
but deliver us from evil.
Amen."**

Can you say the Lord's Prayer by heart?

Give to God

Read these words to your child first:
give   gifts

Jesus saw people give gifts to God.

Read these words to your child first:
money   proud

**Some people gave
lots of money to God.
They put lots of money in a box.
But they were proud.**

Read these words to your child first:
poor   money

**Jesus saw a poor woman
give a little bit of money to God.
She put it in the box.**

Read these words to your child first:

gave   **rich**

**Jesus said,
"She gave more than the rich people.
She gave all she had."**

Why do you think the poor woman gave her
money to God?

Obey My Words

Read these words to your child first:
rock   storm

**Jesus said,
"If you obey my words,
you are like a wise man.
He made a house on rock.
A storm came.
The house did not fall down."**

Read these words to your child first:
foolish **sand**

**"If you do not obey my words,"
said Jesus.
"You are like a foolish man.
He made a house on sand.
A storm came. His house fell down!"**

Would you like to be wise or foolish?

Help Others

Read these words to your child first:
story   left

Jesus told a story:
One day a man went for a walk.
Bad men hit him.
They left him to die.

Read these words to your child first:
came   help

**A man came by.
He did not stop.
He did not help.**

Read these words to your child first:
Another   came

Another man came by.
He did not stop.
He did not help.

Read these words to your child first:
stranger   helped

**A stranger saw the hurt man.
He stopped.
He helped.
"Be like the last man," said Jesus.
"Help other people."**

Why does Jesus want you to be like the last man?

Lost and Found

Read these words to your child first:
story   money

Jesus told a story:
"Give me money,"
a son said to his dad.
"I want to go."
He got the money.
He went and went and went.

Read these words to your child first:
hungry   care

Soon he had no money.
He was hungry.
He took care of pigs
and ate pig food.
"I will go to my dad," he said.

Read these words to your child first:
kissed   work

His dad saw him.
His dad ran to him and kissed him.
"I was bad," said the son.
"Let me work for you."

Read these words to your child first:
party   found

"No!" said his dad. "Let's have a party!
Bring him a robe.
Bring him a ring.
My son was lost and now he is found!"

Why was the dad happy?

Do the Right Thing

Read these words to your child first:
told   story

Jesus told a story:
A dad told his son, "Go to work."
"No," said the son.
But he did go to work.

Read these words to your child first:
right **wanted**

The dad told his other son, "Go to work."
"Yes," said the son.
But he did not go to work.
"Who did the right thing?" said Jesus.
The son who did what his dad wanted.

What is the opposite of right in this story: left or wrong?

331

God Is Good!

Read these words to your child first:
blind   wanted

"Jesus!" said a blind man.
"Shhh!" said the people.
The blind man wanted Jesus.
"Jesus!" he said. "Jesus!"

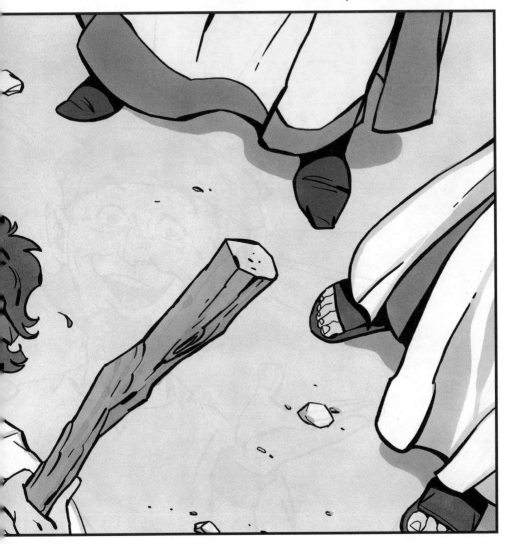

Read these words to your child first:
What   want

Jesus came.
"What do you want?" said Jesus.
"I want to see," said the blind man.

Read these words to your child first:
done   just

**"It will be done
just as you say," said Jesus.**

Read these words to your child first:
people   **they**

"I can see!" said the man.
"God is good!
"He can see!" said all the people.
"God is good!" they said.

Who do you think the man first saw when
Jesus healed his eyes?

Do Good

Read these words to your child first:
breaks   rules

Jesus was good.
But some men did not love him.
They hated him.
"He breaks our rules!" they said.

Read these words to your child first:
seven   heal

"Day **seven** is God's day of rest,"
they said to Jesus.
"We do not work on day **seven**.
Will you work on day **seven**?
Will you **heal** on day **seven**?"

Read these words to your child first:
healed **hand**

**"I will do good on day seven,"
said Jesus.
"That is what God wants."
Jesus healed the man.
Jesus healed the man's hand.**

Read these words to your child first:
were   Let's

The men were mad.
The men were bad.
"Let's kill Jesus," they said.

What part of the man did Jesus heal?

God's Only Son

Read these words to your child first:
good   things

A man went to see Jesus.
"You are from God," he said to Jesus.
"You do good things."

Read these words to your child first:
whoever **believes**

Jesus said,
"For God so loved the world
that he gave his one and only Son,
that whoever believes in him
shall not die but have eternal life."

Can you learn John 3:16 by heart?

The Christ

Read these words to your child first:
drink   know

"Will you give me a drink?"
Jesus said to a woman.
"But you do not like my people,"
she said.
"You do not know me," said Jesus.

Read these words to your child first:
Who   Christ

"**Who** are you?" she said.
"I am the **Christ**," said Jesus.
She was glad.
"Come see Jesus!" she said.
The people were glad, too.

Why do you think the woman told
people to come?

Jesus Healed Him

Read these words to your child first:
could   move

A sick man was by a pool.
If he got in the pool
he could get well.
But he could not move.

Read these words to your child first:
can't   pool

Jesus came by.
"Do you want to get well?"
Jesus said to the sick man.
"Yes," said the man.
"But I can't get in the pool."

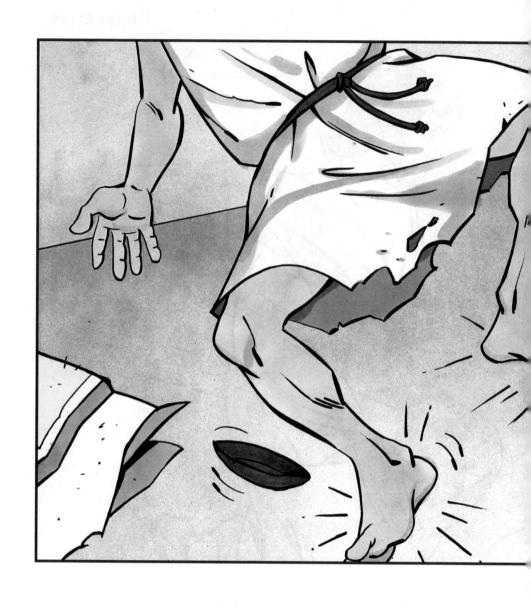

Read these words to your child first:
Pick   walk

**"Get up," said Jesus.
"Pick up your mat and walk."**

Read these words to your child first:
could   healed

**The man got up.
He could walk!
He did not need the pool.
Jesus healed him.**

Did the pool or did Jesus heal the man?

Lots of Food

Read these words to your child first:
hundred   thousand

**Many people went to see Jesus.
Not five people.
Not five hundred people.
Five thousand people
went to see Jesus.**

Read these words to your child first:
hungry   **What**

**They were hungry.
They had no food.
"What can we feed them?"
Jesus said to his men.**

Read these words to your child first:
rolls   fish

A boy had rolls and fish.
Not five thousand rolls.
Not five hundred rolls.
He had five rolls
and two fish.

Read these words to your child first:
Thank   became

**"Thank you, God,"
said Jesus.
Five rolls became lots of rolls.
Jesus fed all the people.**

How did the little bit of food feed so many people?

Be Like a Child

Read these words to your child first:
Does   child

Does Jesus like kids?
Yes!
He said to people,
"Be like a little child
and you will go to heaven."

Read these words to your child first:
love   children

Does Jesus love kids?
Yes!
He said to people,
"Let little children come to me."

What would you say to Jesus if you
could sit on his lap?

Go to Heaven

Read these words to your child first:
What   heaven

"What can I do
to go to heaven?"
a man said to Jesus.

Read these words to your child first:
Obey   else

"Obey God's rules,"
said Jesus.
"I do that," said the man.
"What else can I do?"

Read these words to your child first:
Give   poor

**"Give your money to the poor,"
said Jesus.
"And come with me."**

Read these words to your child first:
money   away

The man was sad.
He did not give his money away.
He did not go with Jesus.
Jesus said, "It is hard to do."

What is the opposite of hard in this story:
easy or soft?

Be Like Jesus

Read these words to your child first:
right   left

"Can we sit with you in heaven?"
said two of Jesus' men.
"Can I sit on your right?"
"Can I sit on your left?"

Read these words to your child first:

choose   great

Jesus said, "I do not choose who sits
on my right or on my left.
But if you want to be great,
help other people like I do."

How did Jesus help people?

Lazarus (say La-zuh-ruhs)

Read these words to your child first:
brother   one

Mary and Martha had a brother.
He was sick.
"Come, Jesus," said Mary and Martha.
"The one you love is sick."

Read these words to your child first:
two   died

But Jesus did not come for two days.
Lazarus died.
Oh, no!
Mary and Martha were very sad.
Jesus was very sad.

Read these words to your child first:
Trust   live

"I am life,"
Jesus said.
"Trust in me and live."

Read these words to your child first:
went   cave

**Jesus went to the cave
that Lazarus was in.
"Lazarus!" Jesus said. "Come out!"
Lazarus came out.
He was alive!**

What did Jesus do for Lazarus?

Jesus' Feet

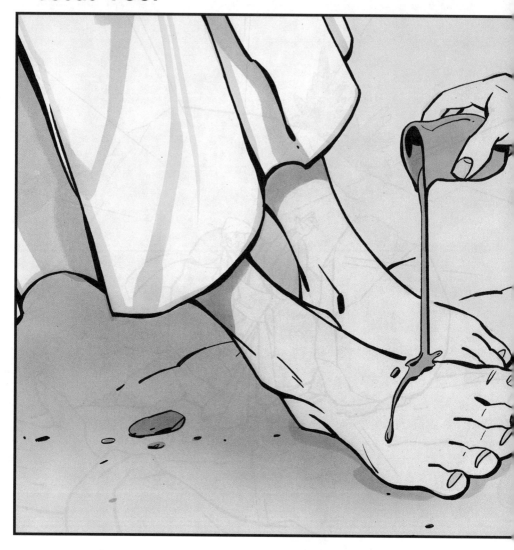

Read these words to your child first:
oil   smell

Mary loved Jesus.
She had oil. It had a nice smell.
She put oil on Jesus' feet.
Mmmmmm!

Read these words to your child first:
wiped   hair

**She wiped the oil with her hair.
Jesus was happy.
"Mary did a good thing for me,"
he said.**

How did Mary show her love for Jesus?

Zacchaeus (say Za-kee-uhs)

Read these words to your child first:
want   short

"I want to see Jesus," said Zacchaeus.
"I can't see him."
Zacchaeus was short.
Very short.
He got up into a tree.
A tall tree.

Read these words to your child first:
Come   down

**Jesus came by.
He said, "Come down.
I want to go to your house."**

Read these words to your child first:
house people

"My house?" said Zacchaeus.
"His house?" said the people.
"But he is bad," they said.

Read these words to your child first:
sorry **being**

**"Jesus, I am so glad to see you,"
said Zacchaeus.
"I am sorry for being bad.
Now I will be good."
Jesus was glad.**

Why did Zacchaeus climb up the tree?

Hosanna! (say Ho-zan-nuh)

Read these words to your child first:
rode   donkey

Jesus rode on a donkey.
He rode it into town.
People were glad to see Jesus.

Read these words to your child first:
branches **Hosanna**

"He is King," they said.
They put branches on the road.
"He is Lord," they said.
"Hosanna!" "Hosanna!"

What kind of tree branches are the
people holding?

371

God's Plan

Read these words to your child first:
away   die

"Soon I will go away,"
Jesus said to his men.
"I will die.
Then I will come back."

Read these words to your child first:
Then   This

**"You will be sad," Jesus said to his men.
"Then you will be happy."
This was God's plan.**

How do you think Jesus' men felt when
Jesus told them he would leave?

Supper

Read these words to your child first:
supper   **bread**

Jesus and his men had supper.
Jesus took the bread.
He said, "Thank you" to God.
They ate the bread.

Read these words to your child first:
drank   remember

Jesus took the cup.
He said, "Thank you" to God.
They drank from the cup.
Jesus said, "Do this to remember me."

Why do you think this is called The Last Supper?

375

A Big Prayer

Read these words to your child first:
with   prayed

"Pray with me," Jesus said to his men.
He was sad that he would die.
Jesus prayed
and prayed
and prayed.
Did Jesus' men pray with him?

Read these words to your child first:
done   coming

No. They went to sleep.
"Let your will be done,"
Jesus said to God.
"Get up," Jesus said to his men.
Bad men were coming.

What does "Let your will be done" mean?

377

Read these words to your child first:
took   away

Jesus was good.
Very good.
But bad men got Jesus.
Bad men took Jesus away.

Read these words to your child first:
perfect   ruler

**Jesus was perfect!
But the bad men said,
"He is not good."
"Kill him!" said the people.
"Kill him," said the ruler.**

What does perfect mean?

379

Jesus Died

Read these words to your child first:
Father   forgive

Bad men hurt Jesus.
Bad men put him on a cross.
Jesus said, "Father, forgive them."
Then he died.

Read these words to your child first:
killed   died

**God's Son was killed.
But God had a plan.
It was a good plan.
Jesus died for our sins.**

What does it mean that Jesus died for our sins?
Hint: See page 438.

Can It Be True?

Read these words to your child first:
tomb   women

**Two of Jesus' men took
his body and put it in a tomb.
Later, two women went to the tomb.**

Read these words to your child first:
angel   alive

**The women saw an angel.
The angel said, "Jesus is alive."
The women ran to tell Jesus' men.
Jesus is alive!**

How did Jesus come back to life?

It Is True!

Read these words to your child first:
saw   talked

**Mary saw Jesus.
She talked to him.
Jesus is alive!**

Read these words to your child first:
true **alive**

It is true.
It is true!
Jesus is alive.

What is the opposite of dead?

Peace!

Read these words to your child first:
said   Jesus'

"Can it be true?"
said Jesus' men.
"Is Jesus alive?"

Read these words to your child first:
sudden   ate

**It is true! It is true!
All of a sudden
Jesus was with them.
He ate some fish.**

Did Jesus eat fish because he was hungry or to
show that he was not a ghost?

Lots of Fish!

Read these words to your child first:
away   fishing

Jesus went away.
His men went fishing.
They did not get any fish.

Read these words to your child first:
back   there

**Jesus came back.
"Put your net there," he said.
They got lots of fish!
Jesus was with them.**

How do you think Jesus' men felt about
Jesus being back?

Jesus Will Come Back

Read these words to your child first:
Holy   Spirit

**Jesus said,
"Tell people about me.
My Holy Spirit will help you."**

Read these words to your child first:
door   die

And then Jesus left.
Did he go out the door?
No.
Did he die?
No.

Read these words to your child first:
sky   with

Jesus went up.

Up.

Up.

Up.

Jesus went up in the sky.

He went to be with God.

Read these words to your child first:
How   angels

Will Jesus come back?
Yes.
How do we know?
Two angels said so!

What is the opposite of down?

Dorcas (say Dor-kuhs)

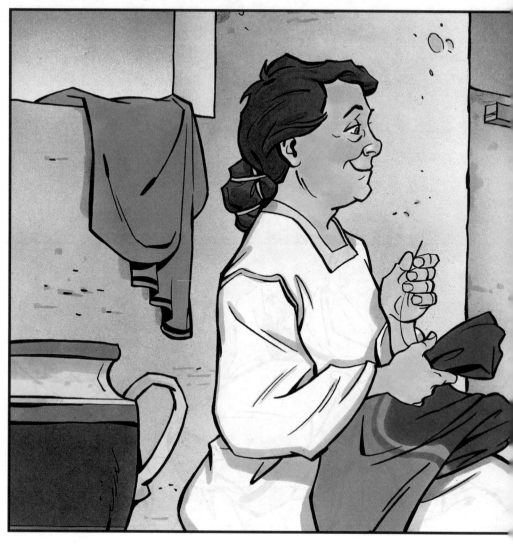

Read these words to your child first:
clothes   poor

Dorcas loved Jesus.
She made lots of clothes
to help the poor.

Read these words to your child first:
Dorcas   died

Dorcas got sick.
Very sick.
Dorcas got sick and died.

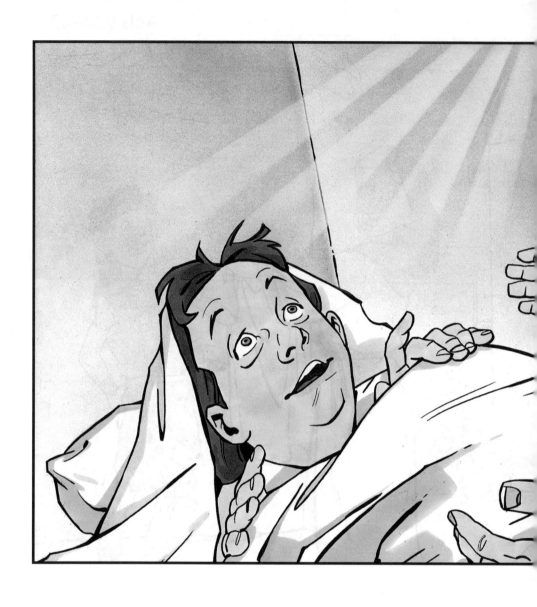

Read these words to your child first:
Come   Peter

"Come, Peter," people said.
Peter was Jesus' man.
"Dorcas died. Come!"
And Peter came.

Read these words to your child first:
prayed   Dorcas

Peter prayed to Jesus.
He said, "Get up, Dorcas."
Dorcas got up.
More people loved Jesus.

Who did Peter pray to?

More Food

Read these words to your child first:
Holy   Spirit

"Soon there will be no food,"
said God's man.
"The Holy Spirit told me."
Oh, no!

Read these words to your child first:
money   more

"We will help," said Jesus' men.
They sent money.
They sent money to get food.
And more people loved Jesus.

Why did Jesus' men help?

Peter (say Pee-ter)

Read these words to your child first:
loved   jail

Peter loved Jesus.
"Do not love Jesus,"
said some bad men.
They put Peter in jail.
But God had a plan.

Read these words to your child first:
friends   prayed

Peter's friends prayed.
"Please, God," they said,
"help Peter."
God sent an angel
to get Peter out of jail.

Read these words to your child first:
friends'   house

Peter went to his friends' house.
"I am here," he said.
"Can it be Peter?" they said.

Read these words to your child first:
Nothing   **hard**

**"It is," said Peter.
"Nothing is too hard for God."**

Will you pray for a friend today?

Saul

Read these words to your child first:
know   better

Saul did not know Jesus yet.
"I will put Jesus' people in jail," said Saul.
But Jesus had a better plan for Saul.
Jesus said, "Saul, Saul."
"Yes, Jesus?" said Saul.

Read these words to your child first:
new   Paul

Now Saul loved Jesus.
He loved Jesus' people.
He was a new man.
Saul's new name was Paul.

Do you think Paul put Jesus' people in jail?
Hint: He is no longer Saul.

Paul Went

Read these words to your child first:
people   that

**Jesus said to Paul,
"Go tell all people
that I am Lord."
Paul went and went and went.**

Read these words to your child first:
told   Lord

**Paul told lots of people,
"Jesus is Lord."
And more people loved Jesus.**

Do you know that Jesus is Lord?

Jesus Is Lord

Read these words to your child first:
could   walk

"Jesus is Lord," said Paul.
"Yes," said a man.
The man could not walk.

Read these words to your child first:
Stand   stood

"Stand up," said Paul.
The man stood up.
Now he could walk!

Read these words to your child first:
people   Paul

**The people saw this.
"You are a god!"
they said to Paul.**

Read these words to your child first:
came   Lord

**"No, no," said Paul.
"I came to tell you,
'Jesus is Lord.'"**

Did the lame man believe that Jesus is Lord?

Good Women

Read these words to your child first:
some   women

**Many people did not know Jesus.
"Jesus is Lord,"
Paul said to some women.**

Read these words to your child first:
more   people

"Yes," they said.
"Jesus is Lord."
And more people loved Jesus.

Do you think Paul liked to tell people
that Jesus is Lord?

Sing in Jail

Read these words to your child first:
Paul   **jail**

"**Paul** loves Jesus,"
said some bad men.
They put **Paul** in **jail**.

Read these words to your child first:
That's   okay

"That's okay," said Paul.
"We can sing to God."
And they did.

Read these words to your child first:
shook   away

God shook the jail.
Paul was free!
Did he run away?

Read these words to your child first:
stayed   **jailer**

No!
He stayed.
He told the jailer, "Jesus is Lord."
The jailer said, "Yes."
And the jailer loved Jesus.

What do you think a jailer does?

Do Not Stop

Read these words to your child first:
Some   words

**Some people
did not like Paul.
They did not like his words.**

Read these words to your child first:
night   afraid

**One night Jesus said to Paul,
"Do not be afraid.
Tell people that I am Lord."
So Paul did.**

Did Paul obey or disobey Jesus?

A Storm

Read these words to your child first:
boat   storm

Paul got on a boat.
Other men got on a boat.
"Don't go yet," said Paul.
"God says there will be a big storm."

Read these words to your child first:
Hmph   come

"Hmph!" they said.
And they went.
Did the storm come?
Yes!

Read these words to your child first:
says   time

Paul said,
"Do as God says
and no one will die."
Did they say, "Hmph?"
No. Not this time.

Read these words to your child first:
They   what

They did what God said.
God was with them.
And no one died.

What happened when they obeyed God?

Paul's Letters

Read these words to your child first:
jail   saying

Paul was in jail.
Did that stop him from saying,
"Jesus is Lord"?
No!

Read these words to your child first:
wrote   letters

He wrote letters.
He wrote about the Lord.

Why did Paul write letters?

Out of Town

Read these words to your child first:
planned   That

Bad men planned to kill Paul.
They said,
"Paul will die."
That was not God's plan.

Read these words to your child first:
soldiers   safe

**Soldiers took Paul out of town.
Paul was safe!
And Paul told more people,
"Jesus is Lord."**

Do you think God was taking care of Paul?

Go Back

Read these words to your child first:
slave   master

**A slave ran away from his master.
He met Paul.
"Jesus is Lord," Paul told him.
"Yes," said the slave.
"Go back to your master," said Paul.**

Read these words to your child first:
sorry   forgive

**"Go back?" said the slave.
Paul wrote a letter to the master.
"Your slave is sorry," Paul wrote.
"And he loves Jesus.
Will you forgive him?"**

Do you think the slave was afraid to
return to his master?

Many People Help

Read these words to your child first:
only   who

**Was Paul the only one
who loved God?
Was he the only one who said,
"Jesus is Lord"?**

Read these words to your child first:
Many   people

No!
Many people loved God.
Many people said,
"Jesus is Lord."

Why do you think so many people love God?

Timothy (say Ti-muh-thee)

Read these words to your child first:
grew   with

**Timothy grew up with God.
"God is good,"
said his mom.**

Read these words to your child first:
good **grandmother**

"God is good,"
said his grandmother.

Read these words to your child first:
Paul   other

He met Paul.
"Jesus is Lord," said Paul.
"Yes," said Timothy.
"Tell other people that Jesus is Lord,"
said Paul.

Read these words to your child first:
Timothy   **Jesus**

**"Yes," said Timothy.
"God is good
and Jesus is Lord."**

What did Paul ask Timothy to do?

Read these words to your child first:
wrote   **heaven**

Jesus' man wrote a letter:
God will make a new heaven.
No one will be sad.
This is God's plan.

Read these words to your child first:
forever   great

**Jesus will come back.
He will take us to heaven.
We will live with him forever.
This is a great plan!**

What do you think heaven will be like?

437

God's Plan for You

God is good.
God loves you.
And he has a plan:
He will let Jesus
take away your sins.
He will let you
live with him forever.

Jesus died
so that we will not be punished.
Jesus lives
and we will praise him.

Do you want to be part of God's plan?
You can!
Say this prayer:

Dear Jesus,
I love you.
I am sorry that I do bad things.
Please forgive me.
Please stay in my life.
Thank you.
Amen

Jesus heard your prayer.
He will help you to love God
and to love others
and to do good things.

My name is...

Today's date.....................................

I asked Jesus into my life.
This is a picture of me asking
Jesus into my life.
(Draw a picture of yourself.)

Now tell someone about your prayer!

Learn-to-Read
BIBLE

Faith Parenting Guide

Levels 1 & 2

Reader

Devotion

Life Issue: I want my children to develop a relationship with God.

Spiritual Building Block: Devotion

Do the following activities to help your children walk with God:

Sight: Ask your child to flip through the pages of the *Learn-to-Read Bible*. Say "Stop," and then have your child point to a person in the picture on that page. Read the person's name and ask your child, "What did God do for him/her?" You might have to give one or two clues. Talk about how God showed his love to that Bible hero.

Sound: Your child will enjoy reading and hearing these Bible stories. Take turns reading pages—you read a page and your child reads a page. When your child wants to know more about a particular story, check the listed reference and read that story from your Bible. You can pray together, asking for wisdom and a closer walk with God.

Touch: Writing helps to improve reading skills. It also helps to keep the idea they learned deep in their heart. Help your child do some writing practice: Model how to write "God" or "Jesus" on lined paper. Help your child to copy it. Praise his/her effort. Read the copied word out loud with your child. Soon your child will be ready to copy phrases such as "God's love" or "God's plan." Ask your child to read the phrase out loud after writing it. Gradually work up to short sentences copied directly from a favorite story in the *Learn-to-Read Bible*. Ask your child to read the written sentences out loud and to illustrate them.

Enjoy this time together with lots of praise and hugs.

Check out the other Rocket Reader books!

The Rocket Reader books are supplemental leveled readers designed to launch children who are learning to read into the wonderful world of words, using biblical concepts.

The five levels each emphasize a different aspect of reading, using level-appropriate language. The books within each set are stored in a durable and attractive slipcover case. Each page is designed to remove intimidating barriers between the new reader and the adventure of reading: only one to three lines are printed on each page, the font is accessible, and the art is engaging and humorous.

Each book includes hands-on faith and reading helps for parents.

Pre-level 1
teaches rhyming and alphabet

Use Rocket Readers Pre-Level 1 if your child:
is a new reader

Heather Gemmen and Mary McNeil

Little Things	0781439817
Rise & Shine	0781439825
Walk This Way	0781439833
Wise Up	0781439841

Level 1
teaches alphabet sounds and beginning sight words

Use Rocket Readers Level 1 if your child:

knows the alphabet sounds

knows how to rhyme

sounds out and reads simple words

Peggy Wilber and Marianne Hering

0781438551   0781438551   0781438608   0781438616

Each title has five books in the set.

Each title has five books in the set.

Level 2
teaches letter combinations and more sight words

Use Rocket Readers Level 2, if your child:

uses phonic skills

knows consonant blends

knows common vowel combinations

Peggy Wilber and Marianne Hering

078143856X   0781438578   0781438594   0781438624

Each title has five books in the set.

Level 3
teaches fluency, more sight words,
and beginning writing skills

Use Rocket Readers Level 3, if your child:

knows common endings

instantly recognizes common sight words

can respond to a story by creating and writing three
simple sentences

Heather Gemmen and Mary McNeil

Something New	0781439868
Spare Me	078143985X
Escape	0781439876
No Fear	0781439884

Each title has three books in the set.

Level 4
teaches comprehension and more
writing skills

Use Rocket Readers Level 4, if your child:

reads fluently at normal verbal speed

comprehends: predicts and summarizes facts of a story

can create a short written response to the reading piece

Heather Gemmen and Mary McNeil

What Will You Be?	0781439779
How Did That Happen?	0781439787
What Will You Do?	0781439795
Who Cares?	

Each title is a 32-page book.